Published by Creative Education and
Creative Paperbacks
P.O. Box 227, Mankato, Minnesota 56002
Creative Education and Creative Paperbacks are
imprints of The Creative Company
www.thecreativecompany.us

Design and production by The Design Lab
Art direction by Rita Marshall
Printed in the United States of America

Photographs by Corbis (Theo Allofs, Jerry Cooke,
Nigel J. Dennis/Gallo Images), Dreamstime (Jenny),
Getty Images (Richard Du Toit, Suzi Eszterhas, Gerald
Hinde, George F. Mobley/National Geographic),
iStockphoto (Dirk Freder, Dieter Hawlan, Emin
Kuliyev, Christian Musat, Thomas Polen, Eliza Snow,
Rick Wylie)

Library of Congress Cataloging-in-Publication Data
Bodden, Valerie.
Giraffes / by Valerie Bodden.
p. cm. — (Amazing animals)
Includes bibliographical references and index.
ISBN 978-1-58341-714-0 (hardcover)
ISBN 978-0-89812-741-6 (pbk)
ISBN 978-1-64000-100-8 (eBook)
1. Giraffe—Juvenile literature. I. Title.
QL737.U56B63 2009
599.638—dc22   2007051585

HC 14 13 12 11 10
PBK 14 13 12 11 10

AMAZING ANIMALS

GIRAFFES

BY VALERIE BODDEN

CREATIVE EDUCATION • CREATIVE PAPERBACKS

Giraffes are tall animals with spots. They have very long necks. There are nine kinds of giraffes in the world.

A giraffe's neck can be eight feet (2.4 m) long

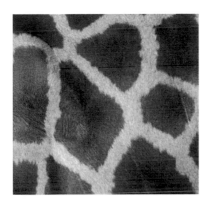

Giraffe fur is the color of dirt and yellow grass

Giraffes have the longest necks of any animal in the world! They have long legs, too. Giraffes have light yellow or white fur with brown spots. Each giraffe has its own **pattern** of spots.

pattern the way something is arranged

Giraffes are the tallest animals on land. If they stood next to a house, they could look in a window on the second floor! Giraffes are heavy, too. They weigh about as much as a car. Even though they weigh so much, giraffes can run fast.

Giraffes can run fast, but they usually walk

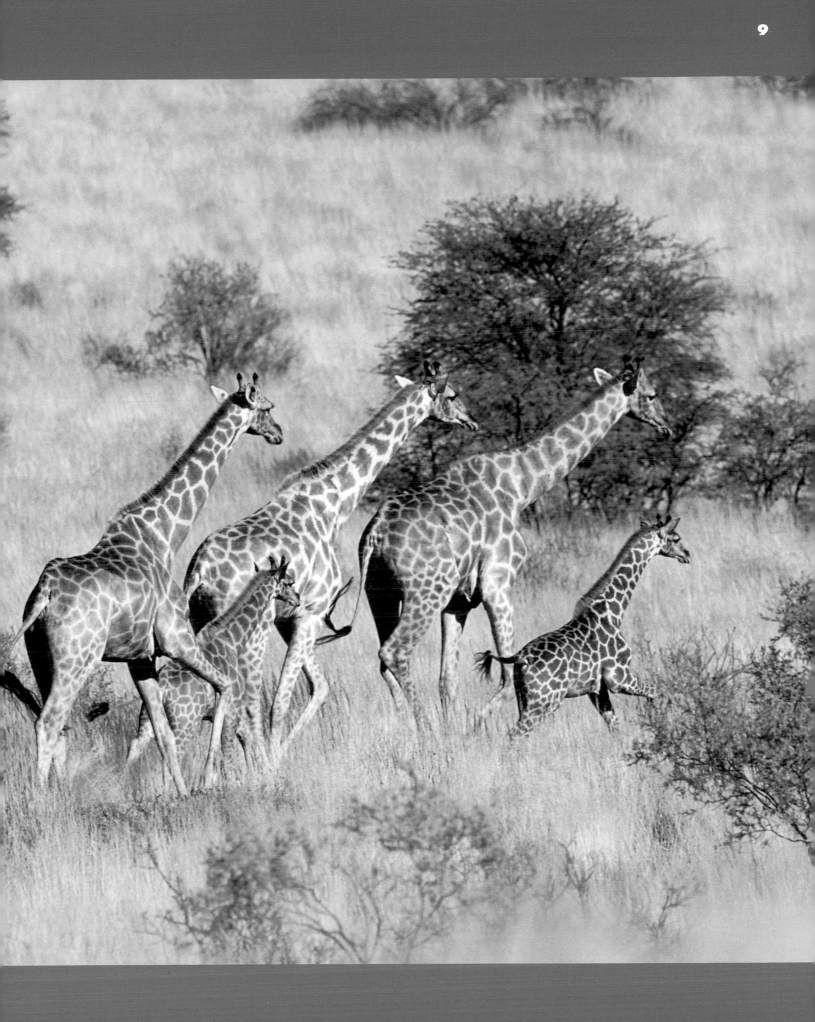

*Africa is a hot continent
with lots of open space*

Giraffes live on the continent of Africa. Some giraffes live in forests there. Others live on lands covered with grass and a few trees.

continent one of Earth's seven big pieces of land

Giraffes eat leaves. They pull the leaves off trees with their long, strong tongues. Giraffes do not drink a lot of water. They get most of the water they need from the leaves they eat.

Giraffes like to eat leaves that just started growing

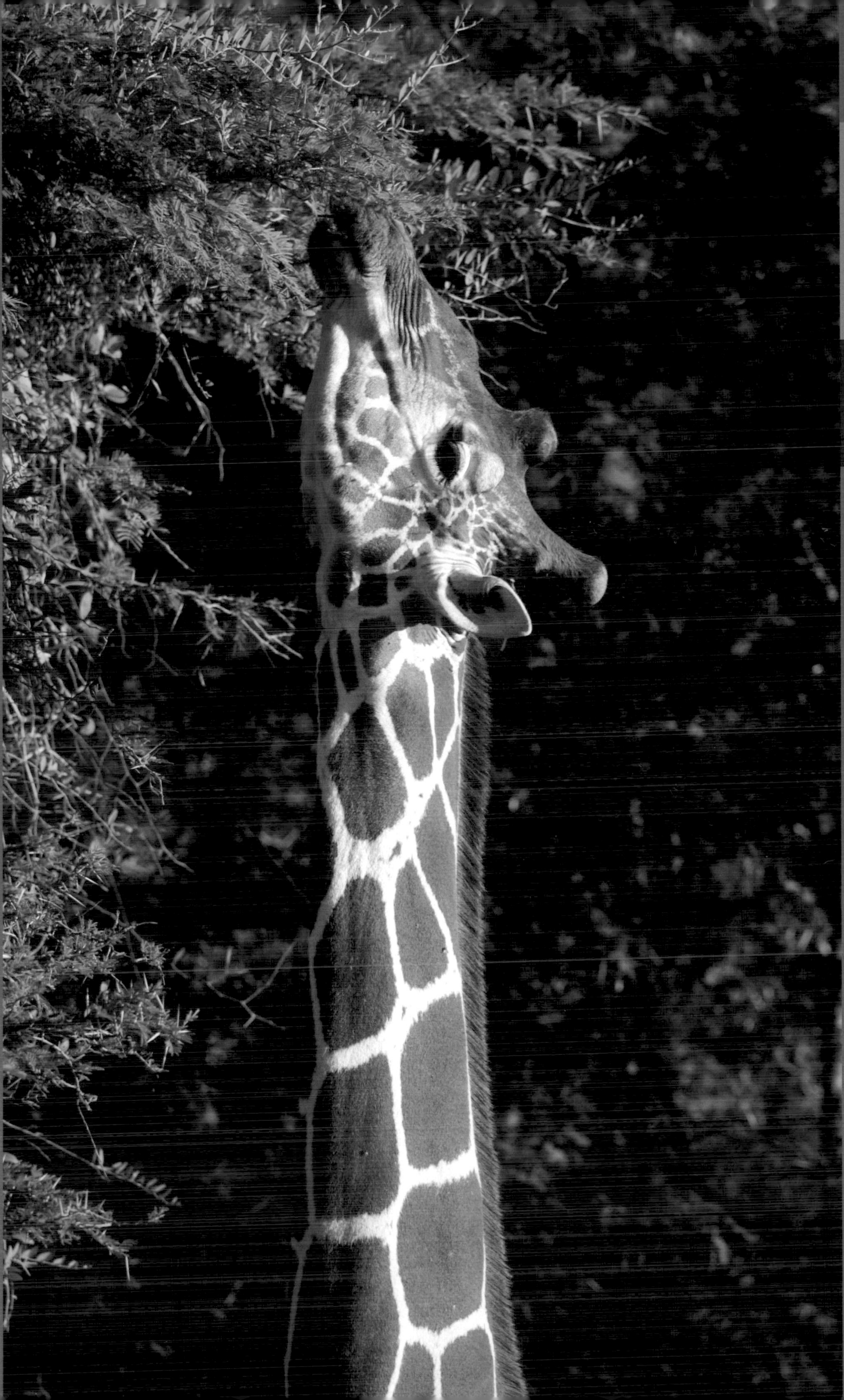

*Mother giraffes always
watch over their calves*

A mother giraffe gives birth to a **calf** standing up. The calf falls to the ground. It is already as tall as a grown-up man. The day after it is born, the calf can run. Wild giraffes can live up to 25 years.

calf a baby giraffe

Giraffe herds watch out for enemies like lions

Giraffes live in **herds**.

About 10 giraffes live in each herd. Giraffes make noises like grunts, snorts, and moos. This is how the giraffes in a herd "talk" to each other.

herds groups of animals that move around together

Giraffes spend most of their time eating. They do not sleep much. When they do sleep, it is for only a few minutes at a time. Giraffes usually sleep standing up.

Giraffes have bumps on their heads called horns

People around the world like to look at giraffes. Many zoos keep giraffes. People can go to the zoos to watch the giraffes. At some zoos, people can even feed the giraffes. It is fun to get close to these tall animals!

People have always liked to see giraffes at zoos

A Giraffe Story

Why do giraffes have such long necks? People in Africa used to tell a story about this. They said that the giraffe once looked like a deer and ate grass. One year, the grass dried up. The giraffe wanted to eat leaves on tall trees. He asked a magic man to make him tall. The man made the giraffe's neck and legs grow very long. Then the giraffe could eat all the leaves he wanted!

Read More

Macken, JoAnn Early. *Giraffes*. Milwaukee: Weekly Reader Early Learning Library, 2004.

Tourville, Amanda Doering. *A Giraffe Grows Up*. Minneapolis: Picture Window Books, 2007.

Websites

Billy Bear's Playground, Animal Scoop: Giraffe
http://www.billybear4kids.com/animal/whose-toes/toes8a.html
This site has giraffe facts, pictures, and movies.

Enchanted Learning: Giraffes
http://www.enchantedlearning.com/themes/giraffe.shtml
This site has giraffe coloring pages and activities.

Index